Don't miss this!

Social Media

Connect with a community of *Bible Studies for Life* users. Post responses to questions, share teaching ideas, and link to great blog content.
Facebook.com/BibleStudiesForLife

Get instant updates about new articles, giveaways, and more. **@BibleMeetsLife**

The App

Simple and straightforward, this elegantly designed iPhone app gives you all the content of the Group Member Book—plus a whole lot more—right at your fingertips. Available in the iTunes App Store; search **"Bible Studies for Life."**

Blog

At ***BibleStudiesForLife.com/blog*** you will find magazine articles and music downloads from LifeWay Worship. Plus, leaders and group members alike will benefit from the blog posts written for people in every life stage—singles, parents, boomers, and senior adults—as well as media clips, connections between our study topics, current events, and much more.

When Relationships Collide
Bible Studies for Life: Small Group Member Book

© 2013 LifeWay Press®

ISBN: 9781415875209

Item: 005600951

Dewey Decimal Classification Number: 303.6

Subject Heading: CONFLICT MANAGEMENT\
INTERPERSONAL RELATIONS \ PROBLEM SOLVING

Eric Geiger
Vice President, Church Resources

Ronnie Floyd
General Editor

David Francis
Managing Editor

Gena Rogers
Karen Dockrey
Content Editors

Philip Nation
Director, Adult Ministry Publishing

Faith Whatley
Director, Adult Ministry

Send questions/comments to: Content Editor, *Bible Studies for Life: Adults*, One LifeWay Plaza, Nashville, TN 37234-0175; or make comments on the Web at *www.BibleStudiesforLife.com*

Printed in the United States of America

For ordering or inquiries, visit *www.lifeway.com*; write LifeWay Small Groups; One LifeWay Plaza; Nashville, TN 37234-0152; or call toll free (800) 458-2772.

HCSB—All Scripture quotations, unless otherwise indicated, are taken from the Holman Christian Standard Bible®, copyright 1999, 2000, 2002, 2003, 2009 by Holman Bible Publishers. Used by permission.

Bible Studies for Life: Adults often lists websites that may be helpful to our readers. Our staff verifies each site's usefulness and appropriateness prior to publication. However, website content changes quickly so we encourage you to approach all websites with caution. Make sure sites are still appropriate before sharing them with students, friends, and family.

We all face conflict.

It can be as simple as two people wanting to sit in the same church pew or as complex as a broken marriage. Conflict is all around us. No one is immune to it. Having conflict doesn't mean two people are spiritually immature or that the conflict will end in broken relationships. As hard as it might be, even in the worst situations, conflict can often be used for an ultimate good. Much of that begins with a proper understanding of conflict.

Thankfully, the Bible never shies away from difficult issues, including conflict. We aren't sheltered from the real messiness of people's lives. The Bible shares with us the good, bad, and ugly of real people, even when they are in the midst of disruptive conflict. We can easily identify with the men and women in Scripture because they often mirror the conflict in our own lives.

Instead of running from conflict, we will discover some principles for dealing with conflict in a healthy, God-honoring way. We will look at the sources and solutions of conflict. If you are in the midst of conflict today, don't despair. God wants to work His will in your life today.

Ron Edmondson

Ron Edmondson, the author of the six-week study *When Relationships Collide*, is a pastor, blogger, and church planter. Ron serves as senior pastor for Immanuel Baptist Church in Lexington, Kentucky. He is passionate about helping people fully grasp the depth of God's love and the power of His grace.

Ron is married to Cheryl, his best friend and the most loving person he knows. Ron and Cheryl have two grown sons who both love Christ and seek to honor and serve Him. Ron loves to read, write, dream, and run. Sometimes he tries to do all of those at the same time.

Ron blogs at *RonEdmondson.com*.

contents

SESSION 1

EVEN CHRISTIANS COLLIDE

What is the silliest argument you've ever been a part of?

Conflict can arise because of different priorities.

THE BIBLE MEETS LIFE

Some of the biggest fights I have witnessed have been over trivial things in a church: paint color, carpet or tile, order of service, whether to buy toilet paper in bulk or as needed. (Not kidding. It happened.) In every situation, Christians were doing the arguing. Most of the time there were two legitimate sides to the discussion, but those involved felt only their opinion was valid enough to defend.

If we step back from the source of conflict in each of the examples above, most of us can see they are trivial in light of the eternal issues the church faces. None of us wants to admit that we get upset about trivial things. They don't seem trivial. But conflict can arise because of different priorities. We want to believe we have our priorities in the right place and we are defending the right positions. Sometimes it takes a 10,000 foot view to help us see what to do. Thankfully, God understands this tension in life and through His Word we have examples of good people who struggled with conflict. The story of Mary and Martha is an example.

WHAT DOES THE BIBLE SAY?

Luke 10:38-42 (HCSB)

38 While they were traveling, He entered a village, and a woman named Martha welcomed Him into her home.

39 She had a sister named Mary, who also sat at the Lord's feet and was listening to what He said.

40 But Martha was distracted by her many tasks, and she came up and asked, "Lord, don't You care that my sister has left me to serve alone? So tell her to give me a hand."

41 The Lord answered her, "Martha, Martha, you are worried and upset about many things,

42 but one thing is necessary. Mary has made the right choice, and it will not be taken away from her."

Key Words

distracted (v. 40) – The Greek word meant pulled or dragged away. It described someone too busy, or overburdened.

worried and upset (v. 41) – The first word was used by Jesus to describe the kind of anxious concern a person might have for food or clothing rather than trusting the Lord to provide (Matt. 6:25-34). The second word literally meant stirred up or troubled.

necessary (v. 42) – That which is a requirement, a requisite, a necessity.

Luke 10:38

Jesus frequently visited homes along His journey. For example, Zacchaeus invited Jesus into his home in Jericho (Luke 19:6). Matthew invited Jesus into his home in Capernaum (Matt. 9:9-13). Simon Peter invited Jesus into his home in Capernaum (Mark 1:29-34). Martha also welcomed Jesus into her home (Luke 10:38).

It is interesting that Martha did the inviting. It would be additional work to entertain Jesus and His disciples. Martha worked to feed and care for the men's physical needs.

We sometimes get the indication from this story that Mary was the more spiritual sister. But what Martha did was incredibly spiritual. She invited Jesus into her home. Hospitality shows God's love. Martha also had a right motive in wanting to serve others. She followed a biblical command to consider other's interests ahead of her own (Phil. 2:4).

Recently, I became pastor of a new church. The people have been overwhelmingly kind to me. When I accept a visit to someone's home, my wife and I are treated almost embarrassingly well. They want to know my favorite foods. They don't want to fix anything I wouldn't like. They prepare their best desserts. I can sit wherever I want to sit. (You know the man has a favorite chair, but it's never even mentioned.) I have to exercise more these days, simply because of their hospitality, but they want to honor their pastor. (They are doing a good job of it.)

> **Which sister do you most relate to? Why?**
>
> QUESTION #1

Most of us go to great efforts to entertain guests in our homes. We can understand why Martha was upset—there was work to be done. Martha was preparing for a suddenly planned visit of 13 hungry and tired men at her house. One of those men was Jesus.

I remember how much my mother loved to entertain. She would invite family, friends, coworkers, and people from church to visit in our home. As much as my mother loved to host people, she always stressed the few days leading up to the event. She wanted things to go well with their visit.

> *How can our responsibilities sometimes be a source of conflict?*

QUESTION #2

STEP BACK

A ministry you're involved in is growing and doing well. But it's causing tension in your personal life because it's taking time away from home.

1. Stepping back and considering God's priorities would affect me by:

   ....

   ....

2. Stepping back and considering God's priorities would affect my home by:

   ....

   ....

3. Stepping back and considering God's priorities would affect my ministry by:

   ....

   ....

Luke 10:39-40

While Martha completed her many tasks, Martha's sister Mary was absent from the kitchen. The connotation I have heard people make is that Martha was the structured, driven personality and Mary may have been a little … shall we say … lazy. We don't necessarily get that from this event. Mary may have been found helping her sister in the kitchen on most days. We do know Mary and Martha often showed unity in their approaches. They both sent for Jesus when their brother Lazarus was sick (John 11:3).

What we see from the event is that Mary, on this particular visit, focused on simply enjoying the presence of Jesus. The phrase, "at the Lord's feet" indicates a posture for learning. She was gleaning from the teaching of Jesus. The customs of the day shunned many women from learning. Women were exempt from studying the Torah. This was a huge opportunity for Mary that she would have few times in her life.

Jesus was probably tired and hungry from traveling and teaching. It would seem inhospitable to ignore His needs or not care for His comfort. Without the help of Mary, Martha baked the bread, set the table, and prepared the meal. She apparently grew more frustrated the longer she thought about her sister sitting rather than helping.

This was a family conflict. There was work to be done to care for the guests. It had to be done if people were going to be properly fed. That was Martha's position. At the same time Jesus was the busy, on-the-go Son of God. He wouldn't be there long. That was Mary's position. Both women focused on good things. The conflict was over noble matters. This isn't a passage about right or wrong. This is a passage about priorities.

Jesus intervened in the conflict and brought a larger perspective.

> *When was a time you had to choose between studying the Bible and accomplishing work that needed to be done?*
>
> *QUESTION #3*

Luke 10:41-42

Often our choices of how we spend our time can cause conflict with others who would make different choices. Our conflict may be with our spouse over how we are going to spend a weekend. It could be with our work over whether to work overtime or go home early. It might be with our own schedule, determining what we can and cannot do with our time.

Every day we make choices based on priorities. That doesn't make the other choice wrong. It doesn't mean we won't have to do all of the choices at some point. It means that in the act of making decisions, it isn't always about right and wrong, as much as it is about good and better.

I have never believed Jesus was criticizing the work we do in the kitchen. I don't believe Jesus is opposed to cooking a big meal or helping guests feel at home. Throughout the Gospels, Jesus enjoyed social engagements. He was frequently found eating. This event at the home of Martha and Mary reminds us we can become distracted with seemingly good things while neglecting things of greater value. That can happen in our careers, our personal time, our family life, and our relationship with Jesus. We need Jesus to give us the big-picture perspective. This may solve much of the conflict we experience.

I like that Jesus didn't ignore Martha's concern. Jesus loved Martha and Mary (John 11:5). Instead of overlooking Martha's concern, Jesus narrowed in on it. Jesus brought perspective to the conflict between Mary and Martha by reminding Martha that, when picking options of how to best spend her time, on this particular day—in this precise moment—Mary chose the better option. Martha was not doing wrongly. Caring for Jesus' physical needs was good. But on this day, sitting to learn from Jesus was the priority.

BEST

What must you consider when you are deciding between good, better, and best?

QUESTION #4

LIVE IT OUT

▶ **Identify what's important.** Evaluate a conflict, looking for what each party considers important.

▶ **Reorder your priorities.** Your stance in a conflict may be good and valid, but it may need to take a temporary backseat to a greater priority.

▶ **Take a half-day retreat.** Do nothing but "sit at the feet of Jesus" in prayer and Bible reading. You will gain a fresh perspective on your other priorities.

The next time an argument arises, step back to see the bigger perspective. **Choose according to Jesus' priorities.**

Fair Game

I've never been the kind of wife to create gourmet meals. I can successfully follow a recipe, but I wouldn't call myself a great cook. Very early in my marriage, I could make about four dishes. Terrell and I ate a lot of chicken and green beans. I also could bake a cake, so there was that. Somehow I perfected homemade potato soup, which quickly became my husband's favorite meal … until the potato soup fight.

To continue reading "Fair Game" from *HomeLife* magazine, visit *BibleStudiesforLife.com/articles*.

My group's prayer requests

_____

_____

_____

_____

_____

_____

_____

_____

_____

My thoughts

SESSION 2

IT'S NOT ABOUT ME

How far are you willing to go to get your own way?

Conflict can arise when I'm thinking only of myself.

THE BIBLE MEETS LIFE

I had a roommate problem when I was in college. I wanted the apartment kept clean; he kept the place messy. I worked full-time, in addition to classes, so I wanted quiet nights. He was a socialite and packed the place with friends. I wanted the window blinds open for natural light. He wanted the blinds closed for privacy. Even as great friends, we created constant tension and conflict for one another.

It wasn't until I was married that I realized why we had roommate problems. As my wife and I built a household and marriage, I recognized a flaw in myself: I wanted things my way. At the heart of much conflict is the desire to get my way. To build a healthy marriage, I often have to drop what I want to take on my wife's desires. I have to consider her interests above my own. She had to do likewise.

Saul and David, two leaders in Israel, lived in conflict because of self-centeredness. In Saul we'll see a man driven by his own self-interests. In David we'll see a man who refused to take a self-centered approach.

WHAT DOES THE BIBLE SAY?

1 Samuel 24:1-15 *(HCSB)*

1 When Saul returned from pursuing the Philistines, he was told, "David is in the wilderness near En-gedi." **2** So Saul took 3,000 of Israel's choice men and went to look for David and his men in front of the Rocks of the Wild Goats.

3 When Saul came to the sheep pens along the road, a cave was there, and he went in to relieve himself. David and his men were staying in the back of the cave, **4** so they said to him, "Look, this is the day the LORD told you about: 'I will hand your enemy over to you so you can do to him whatever you desire.'" Then David got up and secretly cut off the corner of Saul's robe. **5** Afterward, David's conscience bothered him because he had cut off the corner of Saul's robe. **6** He said to his men, "I swear before the LORD: I would never do such a thing to my lord, the LORD's anointed. I will never lift my hand against him, since he is the LORD's anointed." **7** With these words David persuaded his men, and he did not let them rise up against Saul. Then Saul left the cave and went on his way.

8 After that, David got up, went out of the cave, and called to Saul, "My lord the king!" When Saul looked behind him, David bowed to the ground in homage. **9** David said to Saul, "Why do you listen to the words of people who say, 'Look, David intends to harm you'? **10** You can see with your own eyes that the LORD handed you over to me today in the cave. Someone advised me to kill you, but I took pity on you and said: I won't lift my hand against my lord, since he is the LORD's anointed. **11** See, my father! Look at the corner of your robe in my hand, for I cut it off, but I didn't kill you. Look and recognize that there is no evil or rebellion in me. I haven't sinned against you even though you are hunting me down to take my life. **12** "May the LORD judge between you and me, and may the LORD take vengeance on you for me, but my hand will never be against you. **13** As the old proverb says, 'Wickedness comes from wicked people.' My hand will never be against you. **14** Who has the king of Israel come after? What are you chasing after? A dead dog? A flea? **15** May the LORD be judge and decide between you and me. May He take notice and plead my case and deliver me from you."

Key Words

relieve himself (v. 3) – Literally translated as "cover his feet," this expression was a Hebrew idiom for answering the call of nature.

the LORD's anointed (v. 6) – Refers to the anointing process both Saul and David had gone through when God chose them to lead the people. The prophet would anoint them with oil. David refused to go against the Lord's anointing on Saul as long as Saul was alive. He patiently waited his turn to be king.

my hand will never be against you (v. 13) – David pledged he would not lift his hand against Saul, meaning he would never oppose Saul's right to be on the throne.

1 Samuel 24:1-2

David, God's preordained future king, had great success in battle. He became the celebrated hero of the Israelites. Saul, the current king, was angered that his people sang the praises of David's battle victories over his own victories.

Saul's ongoing jealousy and hatred against David led him to pursue David. David went into hiding. Saul's desire to get what he wanted or to have things his way caused pain to himself, to David, and to the kingdom Saul was assigned to lead. While Saul should have been ruling a kingdom, Saul was chasing after David in a rage of anger.

In the previous chapter, it appeared Saul was closing in on David (1 Sam. 23:26). Just when we might believe the end is near, the scales tipped in David's favor.

Life can be like that. Just when I believe all hope is gone, God comes through with a twist of events. I have learned not to consider a life story complete until God puts the period behind "The End."

David was currently the more popular leader. But Saul still had confidants ready to protect him. One of them apparently told Saul where to find David.

It is interesting that Saul took 3,000 of "Israel's choice" men. Powerful king Saul needed 3,000 men to chase a former shepherd boy with limited battle experience. David had a team of misfits as his army (1 Sam. 22:1-2).

But Saul was determined to find and destroy David.

> *What do you do if the person in conflict with you is the one being selfish?*

QUESTION #1

> "Selfishness is when we pursue gain at the expense of others."
>
> —RANDY ALCORN

What are some signs that someone's behavior is out of line?

QUESTION #2

1 Samuel 24:3-7

You can't help but address the humor in this passage. Saul went in the cave "to relieve himself." He had been traveling; there weren't roadside convenience stores along the way; and Saul had to go to the bathroom. It's a poignant reminder that we are all human. Saul was an appointed king of God. He was ruler of a nation. He was the most powerful man in the land. Even so, Saul was merely a human being.

David and his men were in the back of that very cave. It's as if Saul was handed to David on a silver platter. Some opportunities seem so incredibly obvious that we think God must have given them to us.

David secretly cut off the corner of Saul's robe. It is interesting that David's conscience bothered him for this. He had backed away from what he could have done. He could have taken Saul's life. He didn't. So what was so bad? In the customs of the day, cutting off a piece of Saul's robe was symbolic. This was the robe only to be worn by a king. When David cut off a piece of Saul's robe it represented taking a piece of Saul's authority. He assumed power from Saul, which was God's to grant, not David's to grab.

David had been anointed king, but he had not yet been positioned as king. Taking matters into his own hands weighed heavily on David's conscience. The fact that David was led by his conscience showed his character of humility and the influence His relationship with God had on his life.

Consider how your relationship with God alters the way you use your power and influence. David used a good leadership skill here. He persuaded his men not to rise up against Saul. David persuaded his men because it wasn't about him. David was just a man under God's authority.

1 Samuel 24:8-15

Acts of humility are contagious. I've spent the majority of my life in a military town. I was proud to be in the community and to spot a man or woman in uniform. I knew they had sacrificed part of themselves and their family to protect my right to worship freely. No one is currently forced to sign up for this job which puts them in harm's way, makes them face constant deployments, or limits their freedom to choose where they live. People choose to serve through the miliary. It humbles me. The humility of David shows the difference in Saul's approach to leadership and David's approach to leadership:

▶ Saul worked to protect his kingdom. He tried to kill David.

▶ David was able to remove himself from the equation long enough to see a bigger picture.

▶ It might have made sense for David to take Saul's life. Saul was his enemy.

▶ David understood that God was in charge of his destiny.

> **What tempts people to take matters into their own hands?**
>
> QUESTION #3

David's bold pursuit of Saul is humbling. He could have remained hidden in the cave. That could have been the end of the story. It isn't. What David did next is rather amazing. David spared Saul's life without Saul even knowing it.

David had already humbled himself before God and his men. Nothing else was needed. He could have escaped and been safer than before this incident. As a man of God, David felt there was more he needed to do. David felt led to apologize to Saul for usurping part of his power.

In verses like these we see why God might have considered David a man after His own heart. Consider when you've recognized that it's ultimately more about God than about you.

> *What do you find challenging in David's attitude and behavior?*

QUESTION #4

WHAT ABOUT ME?

Your boss offers you a considerable bonus for an idea he thinks you created, but your colleague really did most of the work.

A Christ-centered reaction would benefit me by:

....

....

A Christ-centered reaction would benefit my colleague by:

....

....

A Christ-centered reaction would benefit my family by:

....

....

LIVE IT OUT

The higher we elevate our own needs and desires ahead of others, the more we feed conflict. We get defensive and angry when things don't go our way. Instead, let's elevate God's agenda.

▶ **Don't make the issue about yourself.** Work to see the other person's viewpoint.

▶ **Admit when you've been self-centered.** Acknowledge to the other person where you have erred in the conflict.

▶ **Support the other person.** Even if you have the right stance in the conflict, find a way to tangibly encourage the other person.

Whether it's roommates, spouses, or the person sitting next to you, see how far you can go to make it not about yourself. **Make it about God.**

At Your Service

For me, the journey to a good marriage began with an academic exercise and ended with spiritual renewal. I was a graduate student in seminary, studying to be a pastor and saying to God, "This is not going to work. There's no way I can be this miserable in my marriage and preach hope to people!" Then I thought: "What if I did an in-depth study of the teachings of Jesus and then sought to apply them to my marriage?" In retrospect, it was one of the most profound thoughts I've ever had.

To continue reading "At Your Service" from *HomeLife* magazine, visit *BibleStudiesforLife.com/articles*.

My group's prayer requests

_____

_____

_____

_____

_____

_____

_____

_____

_____

My thoughts

SESSION 3

STAND DOWN

As a kid, what made you call "Mine!" most often?

I don't have to get my way to solve a conflict.

THE BIBLE MEETS LIFE

I recently lost a battle over paint. I gave up. I didn't "win." It wasn't really a battle, but it was tense for a time. And it did involve pain.

In my new church, I encouraged some cosmetic changes to clean up the church in preparation for new visitors we hoped to attract. One day the phone rang. It was someone in the church letting me know about tension simmering over paint colors in a particular room people were painting. The problem was that this particular room had history. No one disagreed that the room needed painting. But the color I chose, in the opinion of one group of people, took away from the history and purpose of the room. In discussing this with someone I trusted, it became apparent that if we stuck with this color, good things we were doing in the church would be usurped.

I have learned there are battles to fight and battles to let go of. I saw this as one to let go. It protected my relationship with the concerned group and healthy growth of the church continued.

Lesson learned: I don't have to get my way to solve a conflict.

WHAT DOES THE BIBLE SAY?

Genesis 13:1-18 *(HCSB)*

1 Then Abram went up from Egypt to the Negev—he, his wife, and all he had, and Lot with him. 2 Abram was very rich in livestock, silver, and gold. 3 He went by stages from the Negev to Bethel, to the place between Bethel and Ai where his tent had formerly been, 4 to the site where he had built the altar. And Abram called on the name of Yahweh there. 5 Now Lot, who was traveling with Abram, also had flocks, herds, and tents. 6 But the land was unable to support them as long as they stayed together, for they had so many possessions that they could not stay together, 7 and there was quarreling between the herdsmen of Abram's livestock and the herdsmen of Lot's livestock. At that time the Canaanites and the Perizzites were living in the land.

8 Then Abram said to Lot, "Please, let's not have quarreling between you and me, or between your herdsmen and my herdsmen, since we are relatives. 9 Isn't the whole land before you? Separate from me: if you go to the left, I will go to the right; if you go to the right, I will go to the left." 10 Lot looked out and saw that the entire Jordan Valley as far as Zoar was well watered everywhere like the LORD's garden and the land of Egypt. This was before the LORD destroyed Sodom and Gomorrah. 11 So Lot chose the entire Jordan Valley for himself. Then Lot journeyed eastward, and they separated from each other. 12 Abram lived in the land of Canaan, but Lot lived in the cities of the valley and set up his tent near Sodom. 13 Now the men of Sodom were evil, sinning greatly against the LORD.

14 After Lot had separated from him, the LORD said to Abram, "Look from the place where you are. Look north and south, east and west, 15 for I will give you and your offspring forever all the land that you see. 16 I will make your offspring like the dust of the earth, so that if anyone could count the dust of the earth, then your offspring could be counted. 17 Get up and walk around the land, through its length and width, for I will give it to you." 18 So Abram moved his tent and went to live near the oaks of Mamre at Hebron, where he built an altar to the LORD.

Key Words

Abram (v. 1) – This was his name before God gave him the covenant name of Abraham (Gen. 17:5).

called on the name of (v. 4) – This expression was first used for worship in Genesis 4:26 and also in Genesis 13:4. It means to acknowledge God by worshiping Him.

quarreling (v. 7) – The Hebrew word used here described a public legal dispute or strife between two hostile parties. Although the word's original meaning related to physical conflict, it most frequently described a verbal dispute.

Genesis 13:1-7

A man named Abram had a conflict to solve. Due to a famine, Abram went to Egypt (Gen. 12:10). Fearing the Pharaoh, Abram asked his wife Sarai to pretend she was his sister. Pharaoh took Sarai into his palace, made her his wife, and made Abram a wealthy man. Pharaoh showered Abram with flocks, herds, and slaves. Abram's sending his wife to live with another man, of course, did not meet God's approval. God brought severe plagues on Pharaoh's household. Pharaoh sent Abram and Sarai on their way.

Abram surely learned that his behavior in Egypt was a mistake. He gained at the expense of his wife.

Abram traveled from Egypt to a new land. On that journey he came back to calling on God (13:4). Abram visited an altar he had built before. At this altar, Abram recognized God alone as His provider. At this altar of God, Abram humbly worshipped God.

I find after a time of worship that I look at things differently. I think Abram must have as well.

Soon Abram faced a new problem. His household and that of his nephew Lot were traveling together. The abundance of Abram's and Lot's possessions caused a problem. There were too many people and livestock with not enough land and resources to support them (13:5-7). Abram sought a solution.

When has a time of worship changed your perspective or course of action?

QUESTION #1

Genesis 13:8-13

I love the maturity of Abram here: "Please, let's not have quarreling between you and me."

Abram's words are a picture of what faith should produce in a believer. Humility arises in the heart of a Christ follower and asks:

▶ "What's God's way of solving this?"

▶ "What's most important here?"

▶ "What's the greater answer to this conflict?"

The best option may be to put aside our interests and let the other person win. It's natural to hold out for what we want. When conflict occurs, even when trying to preserve relationships, we tend to think, *If I don't look after my own interests, who will?* Compromise can be an option. But when we consider the interest of others we can receive the greater benefit of strengthening relationships.

The time may come to part in Christian love. Sometimes when two Christians can't agree—and they have honorably discussed these differences—God may lead them to move apart. That reflects the action Abram took. We see a similar approach between Paul and Barnabas when they couldn't come to an agreement (Acts 15:36-41). Biblical truth should never be compromised in this process.

Abram ultimately gained far more than he sacrificed. Abram's intentionality is an example of Jesus, who seemed to give up everything. Jesus allowed Himself to be arrested and did not defend Himself. His seemingly defenseless position, however, achieved the salvation of all who believe in Him.

> *What keeps us from approaching conflict the way Abram did?*

QUESTION #2

Choose one of these situations and identify your choice

THE **CIRCUMSTANCE**	MY **CHOICE**
1. You'd rather drive straight through, stopping only for gas. One in your group wants to stop for leisurely meals.	If I demand my way, I will: .... If I stand down, I will: ....
2. Your fellow committee member is determined to get his way; solving the problem seems secondary.	If I demand my way, I will: .... If I stand down, I will: ....
3. You and your spouse are both overspending the budget. You blame each other for the lack of funds.	If I demand my way, I will: .... If I stand down, I will: ....

How could your willingness to take the short end of the stick impact your relationships?

QUESTION **#3**

Genesis 13:14-18

God told Abram to "walk around the land, through its length and width" (v. 17). It appears God wanted Abram to enjoy the provision. He wanted him to know what he'd gotten. It's interesting that, according to these verses, there's nothing wrong with having large amounts of land or masses of wealth. God appears to "show off" the land to Abram. So if wealth itself isn't the issue, it must be our attitude toward the things we have or don't have that trips us up at times.

Abram humbly offered Lot the very best of the land. In doing so, Abram trusted God to care for him regardless of his current land situation. Abram, the man of faith, knew that if he was to be a man who trusted God he would not be able to rest on his own strength. He would have to rely on God. And God honored that kind of humility and faith.

"Everyone should look out not only for his own interests, but also for the interests of others."

—PHILIPPIANS 2:4

What choices to stand down have you made that had unexpected results?

QUESTION **#4**

LIVE IT OUT

Conflict happens. So what's our plan for handling conflict in a way that honors God?

▶ **Focus on the end result.** Evaluate what really matters in the long run and work toward it.

▶ **Humble yourself.** Listen to the other person and speak with humility.

▶ **Heal a relationship.** Seek out someone who's been a casualty of a conflict with you and reconcile with that person.

Instead of always yelling "Mine!" notice when standing down might be a better choice. **Consider what saying "Yours" could gain for you.**

Deciding Factors

One of the greatest struggles in marriage is decision-making. Visions of democracy often dance in the minds of young couples, but when there are only two parties, democracy often results in deadlock. How can a couple make a decision? The answer is found in one word—submission.

To continue reading "Deciding Factors" from *HomeLife* magazine, visit *BibleStudiesforLife.com/articles*.

My group's prayer requests

My thoughts

SESSION 4

STAND YOUR GROUND

When have you drawn a line in the sand?

Never compromise when the issue is a matter of biblical right and wrong.

THE BIBLE MEETS LIFE

A man in my church called me recently in distress. He has been a member of the same social club for over 30 years. Most recently he has served as program chair. Part of that assignment was to arrange for the weekly invocation at chapter meetings. The club president asked him to refrain from using the name of Jesus in his prayers. The suggestion that he would pray without the name of Jesus caused my church member tremendous frustration. He couldn't believe he was being asked to deny his Savior. He came to me seeking advice.

What is your non-negotiable? Where will you refuse to compromise?

Paul, an apostle who encouraged believers not to judge someone on issues such as what to wear, what to eat, or how they practiced the Sabbath (Col. 2:16) was vehement on issues of truth. He was willing to face conflict to defend matters of grace to a culture and people that was very attached to the law.

WHAT DOES THE BIBLE SAY?

Galatians 2:1-14 *(HCSB)*

1 Then after 14 years I went up again to Jerusalem with Barnabas, taking Titus along also. 2 I went up according to a revelation and presented to them the gospel I preach among the Gentiles—but privately to those recognized as leaders—so that I might not be running, or have run the race, in vain. 3 But not even Titus who was with me, though he was a Greek, was compelled to be circumcised. 4 This issue arose because of false brothers smuggled in, who came in secretly to spy on the freedom that we have in Christ Jesus, in order to enslave us. 5 But we did not give up and submit to these people for even an hour, so that the truth of the gospel would be preserved for you.

6 Now from those recognized as important (what they really were makes no difference to me; God does not show favoritism)—they added nothing to me. 7 On the contrary, they saw that I had been entrusted with the gospel for the uncircumcised, just as Peter was for the circumcised, 8 since the One at work in Peter for an apostleship to the circumcised was also at work in me for the Gentiles. 9 When James, Cephas, and John, recognized as pillars, acknowledged the grace that had been given to me, they gave the right hand of fellowship to me and Barnabas, agreeing that we should go to the Gentiles and they to the circumcised. 10 They asked only that we would remember the poor, which I made every effort to do.

11 But when Cephas came to Antioch, I opposed him to his face because he stood condemned. 12 For he regularly ate with the Gentiles before certain men came from James. However, when they came, he withdrew and separated himself, because he feared those from the circumcision party. 13 Then the rest of the Jews joined his hypocrisy, so that even Barnabas was carried away by their hypocrisy. 14 But when I saw that they were deviating from the truth of the gospel, I told Cephas in front of everyone, "If you, who are a Jew, live like a Gentile and not like a Jew, how can you compel Gentiles to live like Jews?"

Key Words

Greek (v. 3) – The word designated a non-Jewish person (a Gentile) who spoke the Greek language, observed Greek customs, and absorbed Greek learning. To Jews, Greeks were pagans.

circumcised (v. 3) – Jews removed the foreskin of a male's genital as a sign of membership in God's covenant community. Jews were required to perform the rite on all Jewish male babies.

Cephas (v. 9) - The Aramaic word for "rock," referring to Peter.

right hand of fellowship (v. 9) – The gesture of shaking right hands was used to ratify a covenant.

Galatians 2:1-5

For many of us, our preferred way of dealing with conflict is not to deal with it at all. We ignore it and hope the conflict goes away on its own. While there are some conflicts that may be minor enough to dissipate on their own, many do not. There are conflicts we should walk away from, in the sense of letting go of what we want in the matter (as we saw in last week's study). However, there are some issues on which we should not compromise by giving in, walking away, or ignoring. When conflict is due to an issue of right and wrong, it's time to stand our ground.

When I read the tenacity of Paul in the midst of adversity, I am reminded of two things:

1. Paul was passionate about what he believed.
He was willing to stand the test of time in support of truth. Paul didn't go to Jerusalem because he loved to travel. Paul was on a mission. He went "according to a revelation." Having a clearly defined purpose changes a person's willingness to defend it. Paul knew what God wanted him to do and so he willingly suffered to see the mission of the gospel grow.

2. God knew what He was doing. God called Paul from the diligence he gave to his work against Christ to a passion for Christ. The commitment Paul used to persecute Christians was the same commitment God sought in Paul for the advance of the gospel. God uses the experiences, heart, and temperament of people for Kingdom purposes.

> *How would you describe the freedom we have in Christ?*
>
> QUESTION **#1**

After Paul's conversion, he became passionate about the faith he held in Christ. Nothing could or would stop him from advancing the cause of Christ into the Gentile world. Perhaps no one demonstrates like Paul a commitment to the gospel regardless of the personal cost.

Galatians 2:6-10

Everyone needs people who believe in them. Children need parents who believe in them. Players need coaches who believe in them. Writers need a publisher who believes in them. Pastors need a congregation who believes in them.

Paul needed fellow followers of Christ who believed in him. He had plenty of people who didn't believe in him. He had come from "the other side." He was the chief prosecutor of everything Christian before God miraculously called him into service for the Kingdom. Paul may have felt at times that he had more enemies than he had friends in the church. His work of reaching the Gentiles was unpopular at best. To some it was a cause for hatred, dismissal, and even a sentence of death.

God used men like Barnabas, James, Cephas, and John to encourage Paul in his work. Would he have been as successful without their belief in him? Who has God used in your life to encourage you? Who are you encouraging?

"Be sure you put your feet in the right place, then stand firm!"

—ABRAHAM LINCOLN

Why was it significant that these men gave Paul their support and approval?

QUESTION #2

Galatians 2:11-14

As a pastor, I have learned there are power brokers in the church who carry a tremendous amount of influence. Some of these are helpful. Some are divisive. Cephas (Peter) had good influence sometimes, and not so good influence other times. Paul opposed him to his face.

Peter, perhaps as much or more than the other disciples, was a power broker among the early church. He was in the inner circle with Jesus. Peter was the one to step out of the boat and walk on water. He was ready to cut off an ear in defense of Jesus (John 18:10). Peter denied knowing Christ, but Jesus restored him (John 21). Peter became one of the dominant influencers in the first century church.

It was brave of Paul to stand up to Peter. I don't believe Paul did this simply because he was bold, or stubborn, or that he liked to argue. Paul faced the ridicule for one reason: he "saw that they were deviating from the truth of the gospel."

Peter, of all people, should have been willing to extend grace to the uncircumcised. He had been restored in his relationship with Christ. He had received enormous grace. In Acts 10, Peter encountered Cornelius, an event in which God taught him to embrace a Gentile who was a fellow believer. Paul challenged Peter's treatment of the Gentiles. Peter's hypocrisy was having an impact on the other Jews.

Choosing to challenge someone publicly or privately is a difficult decision. As a leader, I normally handle issues of correction in private. Once, however, I had a staff member who was critical of everything anyone said in a meeting. I had talked with this person before on a number of occasions. At some point, I knew I had to address it in a group setting. The group needed a precedent that this was not a tolerated behavior.

Jesus is truth. His presentation of that truth was always immersed in His love for people. Because of Jesus, Paul was on loving mission to defend and promote the gospel. Nothing or no one could stop him from defending the gospel. Salvation is available to all persons through Jesus Christ.

> *How do you know whether you're standing your ground on biblical principles or personal preferences?*

QUESTION #3

THE **CONFLICT** OF COMPROMISE

A married friend confesses to being unfaithful and asks you to keep it a secret.

Keeping the secret would affect me by:

....
....

Keeping the secret would affect my friend by:

....
....

Keeping the secret would affect my church by:

....
....

> *What role does love play in how you stand your ground?*

QUESTION #4

LIVE IT OUT

▶ **Draw the line in the sand.** Determine your non-negotiables and make sure they are consistent with biblical teaching.

▶ **Practice what you preach.** If you're asking someone to live according to a biblical principal, be certain they can see it in your life.

▶ **Call others to stand with you.** Mentor and disciple someone else in embracing biblical teaching.

The goal of any confrontation is to be redemptive. If truth is being compromised or ignored, we should do what is necessary to correct the situation. We should do this in a way that doesn't simply condemn the other person's actions, but instead, leads him or her back to the truth and a closer walk with Jesus Christ. **That's a line worth drawing in the sand.**

Teaching Points

When it comes to rights, we often teach our kids about their own freedom to express themselves however they choose. We encourage them to share their beliefs without fear. But what about a teacher's right to do the same? Have you ever wondered what a teacher can or can't say, especially in terms of shaping your children's beliefs? And does it make a difference if those teachers are for or against your views?

To continue reading "Teaching Points" from *HomeLife* magazine, visit *BibleStudiesforLife.com/articles*.

My group's prayer requests

_____

_____

_____

_____

_____

_____

_____

_____

_____

_____

_____

My thoughts

SESSION 5

STEP IN

How do you respond when you hear "It's none of your business"?

Step in to keep a bad situation from getting worse.

THE BIBLE MEETS LIFE

I will never forget the time a young man in my church made some poor decisions. This boy grew up in the church. His parents were personal friends. He was active in everything the church had to offer. He made good grades, was popular, and had a bright future.

One day at church he showed up with a girl I knew had a bad reputation. His friends even commented that she was not his type. I knew this young man's character and the potential he had. For several months, I observed them together. It appeared the longer they were together, the less interest this young man had in things of God. He seemed to be losing his ability to discern right from wrong.

I knew the parents well enough to know they couldn't be approving of what I was observing, yet they never approached me. Should I get involved? Was this any of my business? Would I lose their respect if they felt I was interfering? What should a pastor or friend do?

The story of Abigail helps us consider how we can respond to the conflicts of others.

WHAT DOES THE BIBLE SAY?

1 Samuel 25:14-17,23-28,32-35 (HCSB)

14 One of Nabal's young men informed Abigail, Nabal's wife: "Look, David sent messengers from the wilderness to greet our master, but he yelled at them. **15** The men treated us well. When we were in the field, we weren't harassed and nothing of ours was missing the whole time we were living among them. **16** They were a wall around us, both day and night, the entire time we were herding the sheep. **17** Now consider carefully what you must do, because there is certain to be trouble for our master and his entire family. He is such a worthless fool nobody can talk to him!"

....

23 When Abigail saw David, she quickly got off the donkey and fell with her face to the ground in front of David. **24** She fell at his feet and said, "The guilt is mine, my lord, but please let your servant speak to you directly. Listen to the words of your servant. **25** My lord should pay no attention to this worthless man Nabal, for he lives up to his name: His name is Nabal, and stupidity is all he knows. I, your servant, didn't see my lord's young men whom you sent. **26** Now my lord, as surely as the LORD lives and as you yourself live, it is the LORD who kept you from participating in bloodshed and avenging yourself by your own hand. May your enemies and those who want trouble for my lord be like Nabal. **27** Accept this gift your servant has brought to my lord, and let it be given to the young men who follow my lord. **28** Please forgive your servant's offense, for the LORD is certain to make a lasting dynasty for my lord because he fights the LORD'S battles. Throughout your life, may evil not be found in you.

....

32 Then David said to Abigail, "Praise to the LORD God of Israel, who sent you to meet me today! **33** Your discernment is blessed, and you are blessed. Today you kept me from participating in bloodshed and avenging myself by my own hand. **34** Otherwise, as surely as the LORD God of Israel lives, who prevented me from harming you, if you had not come quickly to meet me, Nabal wouldn't have had any men left by morning light." **35** Then David accepted what she had brought him and said, "Go home in peace. See, I have heard what you said and have granted your request."

Key Words

Nabal (v. 14) – The Hebrew term means fool or foolish, from a word meaning to be senseless. This probably was not his given name but a distortion or nickname describing him.

The custom of hospitality
In David's time, his request that Nabal supply food was not unreasonable nor considered extortion. Eastern hospitality, and Israelite law, included providing for needy people and outcasts. Sojourners (nomads) had a right to expect others' hospitality.

1 Samuel 25:14-17

"He is such a worthless fool nobody can talk to him" (v. 17). Wow! The word "Nabal" means "fool." It appears Nabal lived up to his name. Have you ever met anyone like that? Can you imagine that being said about you?

David had provided protection for Nabal's flocks in Carmel at no expense. He asked Nabal to return the favor by feeding his men. It was a feast day, so there would have been ample food. It was not an unreasonable request. It would be expected that Nabal would have happily rewarded David's kindness. David's request was legitimate and it would have been in keeping with the customs of the time.

But Nabal was a fool. His name, and the witness of others said so. Proverbs 10 speaks of men like Nabal, fools who die for lack of sense (v. 21) and who find pleasure in shameful conduct (v. 23). Nabal may have taken pleasure in his arrogance and meanness to David. Nabal was clueless to the danger in the conflict he had begun with David.

David was noticeably angry. He sent his men to do battle against Nabal. One of Nabal's servants was evidently a brave young man. He recognized the problem, knew he had to do something about it, and he took action into his own hands. Abigail was informed of the conflict between Nabal and David.

It is highly unusual to see a wife treated so nobly in the Old Testament. Abigail was obviously an exceptional woman. No doubt, this servant felt comfortable going to Abigail with the news. He had certainly seen the ignorance of his master Nabal, but he must have also seen the wisdom of Abigail.

> *What's the difference between tattling and giving someone information to keep a bad situation from becoming worse?*

QUESTION #1

1 Samuel 25:23-28

Abigail was an intelligent woman (v. 3). As much as her husband was foolish, Abigail was wise. In the culture of the day, it is possible that Abigail was married to Nabal because he was "very rich" (v. 2) and could afford her beauty and intelligence. Abigail realized the potential for devastating conflict.

Abigail responded with:

▶ **Humility**

▶ **Respect**

▶ **Diplomacy**

Some may be tempted to criticize Abigail for going against her husband. Abigail showed she was serving a higher authority. God used her to prevent bloodshed.

Abigail reasoned with David, appealing to his moral character and his wisdom. She helped him see the bigger picture of what God was doing. David's future was promised. Abigail also wisely appeased David with food, his original request of Nabal. Finally, Abigail assumed blame for her husband and appealed for David to remain a man of integrity.

Abigail is a great example of a wise peacemaker. She was kind, humble, wise, and even prophetic. Her conciliatory actions protected her husband, her people, and herself. She also kept David from bringing about needless bloodshed.

What prevents us from stopping a "train wreck" in someone's life?

QUESTION #2

What does Abigail's story teach us about how to step in?

QUESTION #3

STEP IN ... OR STEP AWAY

	STEP IN	STEP AWAY	REASON
A co-worker is about to make a decision that will hurt his chance for a promotion.	☐	☐	....
A neighbor is painting his house an ugly color and the other neighbors hate it.	☐	☐	....
Two church members disagree over a church budget issue.	☐	☐	....

1 Samuel 25:32-35

I can't help but wonder if the death of God's prophet Samuel (1 Sam. 25:1) played a part in David's anger and his decision to pursue Nabal. The country was mourning and David was running from King Saul. Whatever the reason, David recognized Abigail was an agent of God's grace in his life.

David's anger was justified. Nabal was a fool. Even so, shedding innocent blood was not the answer. Abigail's humility and wisdom helped David see the error in his solution. He accepted Abigail's resolution to the conflict. As David had extended grace to Saul (1 Sam. 24), David now extended grace to someone who didn't deserve it: Nabal. David is the opposite picture of the stubbornness displayed in Nabal:

▶ He blessed Abigail for her wisdom and advice.

▶ He was open to rebuke.

▶ He was willing to accept wise counsel.

▶ He humbled himself to admit he was wrong and change his course of action.

David is a reminder of the tenderness of heart God seeks in all who serve Him. With her peaceable nature, Abigail was able to restore peace to David's angry heart. Abigail protected David from sinning. She prevented David from taking matters into his own hands. His anger would have caused him to behave more like his predecessor Saul, instead of a "man after God's own heart." Saul lost the kingdom because he sinned against God. David perhaps saw that he had just avoided doing the same and he humbly recanted of his actions against Nabal. Abigail brought peace to more than just her household. Her efforts kept David from fighting Nabal and ultimately protected his future reign as king.

"David accepted what she had brought him" (v. 35). In her effort to bring peace to a mounting conflict, Abigail had not come empty-handed. Forgiveness is based on extending undeserved grace, but sometimes to solve a conflict, justice must be served and wrongs must be made right.

> **What does it take to step in and get involved?**
>
> QUESTION #4

LIVE IT OUT

You remember the young man on page 46? I felt led by God to say something to him. He politely listened to me, but he chose to continue seeing the girl. Later he realized she was not a good fit for the direction he wanted to take his life. He began to make better choices, and today he continues to live his life to honor Christ. Three actions to take when deciding whether or not to step in are:

▶ **Give permission.** Give someone permission to step in if you are about to make a bad decision.

▶ **Seek advice.** If you're not sure if you should step into someone else's problem, ask the advice of someone you trust.

▶ **Intervene diplomatically.** Say what needs to be said with humility and respect.

Let God lead as you step in to keep a bad situation from getting worse.

Not So Fast

Whenever Monty and Carla have a conflict, Carla bolts.

In their first session with Monty and Carla (married one year), Tim and Britney (married 14 years) jumped right in to explain how destructive avoiding conflict can be. "If you run from your problems, Carla, you'll never resolve them— you'll create loose ends that eat away at your marriage," Tim said. "You've got to discuss issues." With that, Carla broke into tears and walked away from the meeting.

To continue reading "Not So Fast" from *HomeLife* magazine, visit *BibleStudiesforLife.com/articles*.

My group's prayer requests

....
....
....
....
....
....
....
....
....

My thoughts

SESSION 6

THE BIG PICTURE

When have you seen the silver lining in a difficult situation?

God is at work even in the midst of conflict.

THE BIBLE MEETS LIFE

My father left my mother, brother, and me when I was six. He came in and out of our lives over the years, but was absent most of my life. He was an alcoholic. When times were good, we had a decent relationship. Those times were rare. It was the largest source of conflict in my life. When I was 12, my father tried to parent me again. I resisted. He persisted. It was a battle of the wills for 25 years or so.

For years, my mother and others tried to encourage the relationship between my father and me. My father, in later years, sobered up, got right with Christ, and completely rebuilt a strong relationship with my mother. Even after I entered the ministry, it was the one relationship bridled with the most conflict, mostly on my part.

What good could ever come from our relationship?

The story of Joseph is one of the strongest examples of family conflict within the Bible. The story holds nothing back. It is messy. Favoritism, hatred, and envy defined Jacob's family. Yet, even in the midst of that kind of family dysfunction, God had a plan.

WHAT DOES THE BIBLE SAY?

Genesis 37:5-8,26-28; 50:15-21 (HCSB)

37:5 Then Joseph had a dream. When he told it to his brothers, they hated him even more. **6** He said to them, "Listen to this dream I had: **7** There we were, binding sheaves of grain in the field. Suddenly my sheaf stood up, and your sheaves gathered around it and bowed down to my sheaf." **8** "Are you really going to reign over us?" his brothers asked him. "Are you really going to rule us?" So they hated him even more because of his dream and what he had said.

26 Then Judah said to his brothers, "What do we gain if we kill our brother and cover up his blood? **27** Come, let's sell him to the Ishmaelites and not lay a hand on him, for he is our brother, our own flesh," and they agreed. **28** When Midianite traders passed by, his brothers pulled Joseph out of the pit and sold him for 20 pieces of silver to the Ishmaelites, who took Joseph to Egypt.

50:15 When Joseph's brothers saw that their father was dead, they said to one another, "If Joseph is holding a grudge against us, he will certainly repay us for all the suffering we caused him." **16** So they sent this message to Joseph, "Before he died your father gave a command: **17** 'Say this to Joseph: Please forgive your brothers' transgression and their sin—the suffering they caused you.' Therefore, please forgive the transgression of the servants of the God of your father." Joseph wept when their message came to him. **18** Then his brothers also came to him, bowed down before him, and said, "We are your slaves!" **19** But Joseph said to them, "Don't be afraid. Am I in the place of God? **20** You planned evil against me; God planned it for good to bring about the present result—the survival of many people. **21** Therefore don't be afraid. I will take care of you and your little ones." And he comforted them and spoke kindly to them.

Genesis 37:5-8

Favoritism, hatred, and envy defined Jacob's family. Apparently it was common knowledge that Joseph was his dad's favorite son (Gen. 37:3).

It is never right to play favorites with children. If a parent has more than one child, each child will be different. We are all "remarkably and wonderfully made" (Ps. 139:14).

Joseph was special in one sense. He had a unique ability to dream prophetically. As we learn from reading further into Joseph's story (Gen. 40–41), not only was Joseph a dreamer, but he also had the ability to interpret dreams. At 17, however, Joseph didn't yet know how to share his dreams in ways that helped.

Recently, some parents came to talk with me about their twin daughters. They couldn't understand why the girls love each other so much but continually fight over issues that are clearly fueled by jealousy. I wanted to be helpful, but realized that part of this was a normal dynamic among siblings, especially those identical in age.

Regardless of the motive, Joseph aroused the envy of his brothers through his words and behavior. His actions were perceived as coming from a self-righteous attitude.

> **When have you seen behaviors like this fuel the fire of conflict?**

QUESTION #1

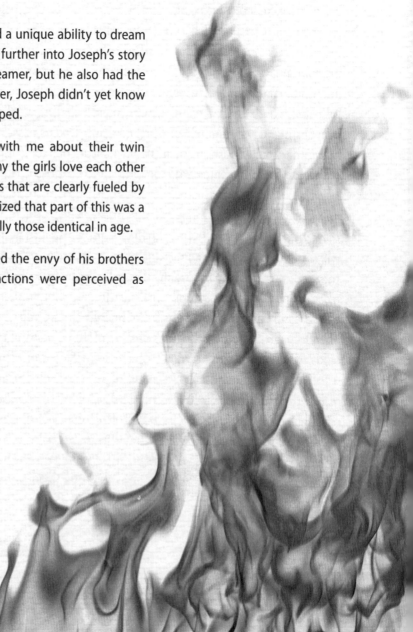

"When a train goes through a tunnel and it gets dark, you don't throw away the ticket and jump off. You sit still and trust the engineer."

—CORRIE TEN BOOM

Genesis 37:26-28

Joseph's brothers, the older sons of Jacob, let their hatred of Joseph grow to the point that they wanted to kill him. They chose instead to profit from their hatred, and sold Joseph into slavery. (I have always wondered what they did with the money.)

In the eyes of society, the brothers were not guilty of murder. Instead of killing Joseph, they opted to sell him. They allowed his father to believe he had been killed.

In the eyes of Jesus, though, the brothers were guilty of murder (see Matt. 5:22). They may have taken a more merciful route, but Joseph's life was severely disrupted by the conflict with his brothers. He would serve as a slave. He would live far from home. He would go to prison. His life would never be the same.

> **How has a conflict shaped your life?**
>
> QUESTION **#2**

Genesis 50:15-21

From the brothers' perspective, it seemed they were done with their brother. Years later, though, they found themselves standing before Joseph as he served as the second-in-command in Egypt. Joseph had learned much over the years. He chose to do the right thing even in the face of incredible injustice.

As Joseph matured, he also learned how to use the special gift God had given him to dream prophetically. He saw the hand of God at work. Joseph forgave his brothers.

This story reminds me that the greatest injustice ever committed was the cruel death of Jesus Christ on a cross. He was perfect, having never sinned. He willingly submitted Himself to being brutally murdered. Those who witnessed the crucifixion, even His closest disciples, could not understand that seemingly senseless death. In spite of that tragedy, God used the death of the sinless One to bring about salvation for all who place their faith in His Son. God was at work in the death of Christ.

We may not always see how God is at work in a situation. It often takes time for the big picture of God's work to be revealed. Just as in the story of Joseph, God's grace leads us to forgive others. When we trust that God is at work in our conflict, we can more easily extend forgiveness to the other person.

The day I chose to forgive my father was one of the most freeing days of my life. It allowed me to build a relationship with my father the last few years of his life. I still have pain in the memories of those years, but God used them for an ultimate good in my life. I can clearly trace my commitment as a husband and father back to my frustration with my own family life as a child. God used those days to confirm the future life he wanted me to have. God does redeem the times, even in the midst of conflict.

> **What will help you extend forgiveness when you're wronged?**
>
> QUESTION #3

The author, Ron Edmondson, with his family.

THE BIG PICTURE

1. A family member who hurt you years ago is now asking to be a part of your life again. However, the very thought of the reunion brings back painful, unresolved memories.

How might God be at work in the midst of this?

....

....

....

....

2. Identify a current conflict in your life. Reflect on your answer over the next few days.

How might God be at work in the midst of this?

....

....

....

....

> *How can we encourage each other when we struggle to see evidence that God is at work in difficult situations?*

QUESTION *#4*

LIVE IT OUT

Conflict can be draining, but God can use whatever conflict we are facing to bring meaningful results in our lives. Conflict can lead to resolution which ultimately can lead to a far stronger relationship. And in the process, God can strengthen our faith and endurance.

▶ **Trust.** Even if you can't see God's hand yet, trust that He is at work.

▶ **Forgive.** Regardless of who's at fault in the conflict, forgive the other person.

▶ **Call.** Contact someone and let him or her know how God changed you because of your experience with the conflict.

Could God be at work in your conflict, preparing a better story for you? **That's far better than any silver lining.**

Love Greater Than Our Sins

Obviously, because I'm a Christian author and speaker who's married to a pastor, our children are perfect, always behaving as if singing angels dropped them straight into our arms from the bosom of heaven. Their first words were, "I want to ask Jesus into my heart." (I know, right? Brandon and I were surprised, too. They skipped right over Mama and Dada to the Gospel of Atonement.) But I've heard of other kids who can be rotten. Ahem.

To continue reading "Love Greater than Our Sins" from *HomeLife* magazine, visit *BibleStudiesforLife.com/articles*.

My group's prayer requests

_____

_____

_____

_____

_____

_____

_____

_____

_____

_____

My thoughts

When Relationships Collide

We have looked at six different relationships in the pages of Scripture, relationships from which we can pull solid principles for resolving conflict. As we strengthen our relationships, the ultimate goal is to develop into people who know Christ and His gracious work, who are contributing servants in the community of faith, and who are effectively engaging the culture without losing distinction.

Christ

Jesus Christ seemed to give up everything He had worked for when He allowed Himself to be crucified. His seemingly defenseless position, however, achieved His ultimate goal: the salvation of all who believe in Him. Sin has placed the human race in conflict with a holy God, yet God provided His Son, Jesus, who willingly stepped in to remove our sin and appease God's wrath.

Community

Relationships are torn apart by self-centeredness. The family and the church are to be Christ-centered. When conflict in the church is carried out with grace and love, problems are solved, the church is strengthened, and the world gets a positive witness of the gospel at work.

Culture

Who am I to call into question what others believe or do? Personal preferences are one thing, but when it comes to truth—clear biblical teaching— we must stand our ground and speak up.

GENERAL INSTRUCTIONS

In order to make the most of this study and to ensure a richer group experience, it's recommended that all group participants read through the teaching and discussion content in full before each group meeting. As a leader, it is also a good idea for you to be familiar with this content and prepared to summarize it for your group members as you move through the material each week.

Each session of the Bible study is made up of three sections:

1. THE BIBLE MEETS LIFE.

An introduction to the theme of the session and its connection to everyday life, along with a brief overview of the primary Scripture text. This section also includes an icebreaker question or activity.

2. WHAT DOES THE BIBLE SAY?

This comprises the bulk of each session and includes the primary Scripture text along with explanations for key words and ideas within that text. This section also includes most of the content designed to produce and maintain discussion within the group.

3. LIVE IT OUT.

The final section focuses on application, using bulleted summary statements to answer the question, *So what?* As the leader, be prepared to challenge the group to apply what they learned during the discussion by transforming it into action throughout the week.

For group leaders, the *When Relationships Collide* Leader Guide contains several features and tools designed to help you lead participants through the material provided.

ICEBREAKER

These opening questions and/or activities are designed to help participants transition into the study and begin engaging the primary themes to be discussed. Be sure everyone has a chance to speak, but maintain a low-pressure environment.

DISCUSSION QUESTIONS

Each "What Does the Bible Say?" section features at least four questions designed to spark discussion and interaction within your group. These questions encourage critical thinking, so be sure to allow a period of silence for participants to process the question and form an answer.

The *When Relationships Collide* Leader Guide also contains optional follow-up questions and activities that may be helpful to your group, if time permits.

DVD CONTENT

Each video features teaching from Ron Edmondson on the primary themes found in the session. We recommend that you show this video in one of three places: (1) At the beginning of group time, (2) After the icebreaker, or (3) After a quick review and/or summary of "What Does the Bible Say?" A video summary is included as well. You may choose to use this summary as background preparation to help you guide the group.

This Leader Guide also contains questions to help transition from the video into group discussion. For a digital Leader Guide with commentary, see the "Leader Tools" folder on the DVD-ROM in your Leader Kit.

SESSION ONE: EVEN CHRISTIANS COLLIDE

The Point: Conflict can arise because of different priorities.

The Passage: Luke 10:38-42

The Setting: As Jesus journeyed toward Jerusalem (Luke 9:51), He stopped at the home of Mary and Martha. While Jesus taught in their home, Martha focused on the duties of a hospitable host, but Mary focused on listening to Jesus teach. Both women were doing good things, but at that moment only one was necessary: to listen to Jesus teach.

Icebreaker: What is the silliest argument you've ever been a part of?

> *Optional follow-up:* What specific "triggers" (events, circumstances, key words, etc.) tend to send you down the path toward a relationship collision?

> *Optional activity:* Display several household items that represent common triggers for conflict. These items could include a TV remote, a checkbook, a garbage bag, a roll of toilet paper, a screwdriver, a pillow, and so on. Encourage participants to pick up different items and even pass them around as you discuss the following questions:

> - Which of these items produces the strongest emotional reaction for you? Why?
> - Which of these items represents a collision point in your family?
> - Why do you think such trivial things can create so much tension?
> - Have you developed a plan for navigating these moments when they surface?

Video Summary: Ron opens the video teaching by talking about how conflict is prevalent even among Christian believers. Conflict seldom disappears on its own. Rather, it requires intentionality on someone's part. He uses the text to point out how Martha and Mary's friendship seemed to help them bear conflict. It's also helpful to point out that Jesus was neither unfamiliar nor uncomfortable with conflict. This helps us understand that God will often use conflict to redirect our hearts to what is truly important. In his video message Ron also says that it's helpful to do some self analysis and recommends two questions to ask ourselves:

- What unresolved conflict is in my life?
- Are there issues I have neglected or hidden in my heart?

WATCH THE DVD SEGMENT FOR SESSION 1, THEN USE THE FOLLOWING QUESTIONS TO TRANSITION INTO THE STUDY.

- The video references a man who had held a grudge for 40 years. Talk about the fallout of unresolved conflict in our lives. What are the dangers and ultimate results of harboring a grudge?

- Ron points out that Jesus is neither unfamiliar nor uncomfortable with conflict. What does this reveal about God and how He might use conflict in our lives?

WHAT DOES THE BIBLE SAY?

ASK FOR A VOLUNTEER TO READ ALOUD LUKE 10:38-42.
Response: What's your initial reaction to these verses?

- What questions do you have about these verses?

- What new application do you hope to get from this passage?

TURN THE GROUP'S ATTENTION TO LUKE 10:38.
QUESTION 1: Which sister do you most relate to? Why?

This question provides a great opportunity for group members to tell their stories, which is important as people seek to reveal themselves to the group. Make time for those stories if they come.

> *Optional follow-up using John 11:18-27*: The same Martha is found in this passage of John. What attributes become evident in Martha's actions and words in this passage?

QUESTION 2: How can our responsibilities sometimes be a source of conflict?

This is an application question that asks group members to consider how not only their own responsibilities, but the responsibilities of others in their lives, might contribute to interpersonal conflict.

> *Optional follow-up:* Scripture illustrates for us that Martha was a passionate person. How do you think attributes that are usually very functional and positive—like passion—can also contribute to conflict?

> *Optional activity:* Draw attention to the exercise labeled "Step Back." You may choose to lead your group through this exercise together or give members a few moments to respond on their own by writing their answers in their books or recording them in the app.

MOVE TO LUKE 10:39-40.
QUESTION 3: When was a time you had to choose between studying the Bible and accomplishing work that needed to be done?

This question requires group members to recall a time when they had to wrestle with priorities, timeliness of responsibilities, and perhaps even how their decision would affect those around them. There are times when we simply need to get a job done and other times that avail themselves more to Scripture reading and study. The decision often comes down to planning and balance. Family members, people with whom we work, and friends deserve our best and prioritizing is an important first step in avoiding conflict.

> *Optional follow-up:* What factors make planning and prioritizing most difficult in your life?

CONTINUE WITH LUKE 10:41-42.
QUESTION 4: What must you consider when you are deciding between good, better, and best?

This is an application question that may result in another opportunity for group members to share their stories. You can encourage this kind of self-disclosure by asking, "When have you rejected something 'good' in favor of what was 'best'"?

Note: The following question does not appear in the group member book. Use it in your group discussion as time allows.

QUESTION 5: Martha was very willing to confront. How do you typically respond when confronted by others?

This is a self-revelation question included to initiate a discussion of conflict and how each of us handles it.

> *Optional follow-up:* Are Christians supposed to respond in a particular way when confronted?

> *Optional follow-up:* Talk about how Jesus, Martha, and Mary all handled this situation. What are some skills and takeaways to be gleaned from this interaction?

LIVE IT OUT

Invite group members to consider both past and present conflict and the effects of unresolved conflict. Point out three lessons learned from Luke 10:38-42:

- **Identify what's important.** Evaluate a conflict, looking for what each party considers important.

- **Reorder your priorities.** Your stance in a conflict may be good and valid, but it may need to take a temporary backseat to a greater priority.

- **Take a half-day retreat.** Do nothing but "sit at the feet of Jesus" in prayer and Bible reading. You will gain a fresh perspective on your other priorities.

Challenge: Encourage participants to be sensitive to those moments with potential for conflict and, in the moment, consider how priorities might influence their actions. Ask group members to take time to journal about the experience and come prepared to share during the next meeting.

Pray: Ask for prayer requests and ask group members to pray for the different requests as intercessors. As the leader, close the prayer time by being the last person to take your petitions and praises to God. Be sure to invite God into every aspect of each life represented in the room where conflict, the potential for conflict, and the origins of conflict are concerned.

SESSION TWO: IT'S NOT ABOUT ME

The Point: Conflict can arise when I'm thinking only of myself.

The Passage: 1 Samuel 24:1-15

The Setting: David hid in the wilderness because Saul sought to kill him. Saul pursued David to the wilderness near En-Gedi. Saul sought relief in a cave in which David and his men were hiding. David had an easy opportunity to kill Saul, but he refused to kill the king. David then made Saul aware of how he had spared his life, using the moment to proclaim his lack of evil intent against the king.

Icebreaker: How far are you willing to go to get your own way?

> *Optional activity:* Lead your group on an in-depth exploration of selfishness in today's culture. To start, ask participants to make a list of selfish personalities portrayed through movies, TV shows, and books. Be sure to keep the group focused on fictional personalities, not real people. Ask for a volunteer to record the list on a whiteboard or large sheet of paper. Once you have a large list, lead the group through unpacking these questions:

- Other than selfish behavior, what do the personalities on our list have in common?

- How do we identify or measure selfishness in today's society? What are the symptoms of selfishness?

Video Summary: Ron opens this video by talking about David and his decision to spare the life of King Saul (1 Sam. 24:1-15). David was destined for success, both as a king and as a leader of God's people. He wasn't just a man after God's own heart, he was a man who received blessing and favor from God. But Ron reminds us that David's story is a perfect illustration of how being a person after God's own heart doesn't mean we won't have trouble.

WATCH THE DVD SEGMENT FOR SESSION 2, THEN USE THE FOLLOWING QUESTIONS OR DISCUSSION STARTERS TO TRANSITION INTO THE STUDY.

- In the video Ron references a friend who was able to demonstrate faith and confidence in God in spite of all the wrongs done to her. Discuss as a group your initial response as Ron shared his friend's story.

- Ron used his friend's story as an example of what God will do in the heart of those who submit to His will. As a believer, how do you respond to conflict when it surfaces in your life?

WHAT DOES THE BIBLE SAY?

ASK FOR A VOLUNTEER TO READ ALOUD 1 SAMUEL 24:1-15.
Response: What's your initial reaction to these verses?

- What questions do you have about these verses?

- What do you hope to gain from studying David's reaction to King Saul in this week's study?

TURN THE GROUP'S ATTENTION TO 1 SAMUEL 24:1-2.
QUESTION 1: What do you do if the person in conflict with you is the one being selfish?

This is an application question designed to lead group members to examine their actions and motivations when confronted with a situation where the other person is not willing to compromise. Guide group members to consider the importance of looking at the big picture. How important is it to stand my ground? Will others be affected? How?

MOVE TO 1 SAMUEL 24:3-7.
QUESTION 2: What are some signs that someone's behavior is out of line?

   Optional follow-up: What does it take for us to observe these signs in our own lives?

CONTINUE WITH 1 SAMUEL 24:8-15.
QUESTION 3: What tempts people to take matters into their own hands?

This self-revelation question will guide group members to examine what is at the heart of their desire to control a situation. Responses will likely indicate feelings such as fear, lack of trust, pride, etc.

   Optional follow-up: When have you been tempted recently to take matters into your own hands?

   Optional follow-up: What are some of the consequences of taking matters into our own hands?

QUESTION 4: What do you find challenging in David's attitude and behavior?

Optional activity: Refer group members to the activity called "What About Me?" in the book. Ask for volunteers to respond to one of the three options.

Optional follow-up: Do you find it easy or difficult to apologize when you know you're wrong? Explain.

Note: The following question does not appear in the group member book. Use it in your group discussion as time allows.

QUESTION 5: Apologies can be loaded with expectations. Why do you think those expectations can make it more difficult for us to say we're sorry?

This question is intended to lead group members to recognize when they carry expectations with them into an apology and how those expectations can make the process more difficult. They may talk about hopes, desires, uncertainties, or even fears related to how their apology will be accepted.

Optional follow-up: How might our motivation to apologize affect these expectations?

LIVE IT OUT

Point out that the higher we elevate our own needs and desires ahead of others, the more we feed conflict. We get defensive when things don't go our way. Instead, elevate God's agenda. Guide the group to choose ways to do this.

- **Don't make the issue about yourself.** Work to see the other person's viewpoint.

- **Admit when you've been self-centered.** Acknowledge to the other person where you have erred in the conflict.

- **Support the other person.** Even if you have the right stance in the conflict, find a way to tangibly encourage the other person.

Challenge: Encourage participants to be open to both sides of a conflict situation, to examine what is motivating their actions and reactions, and to be willing to consider the other person's position, whether right or wrong. Ask group members to take the time to journal about a conflict situation they encounter during the week and come prepared to share during the next meeting.

Pray: Ask for prayer requests and ask group members to pray for the different requests as intercessors. As the leader, close the prayer time by committing the members in your group to the Lord and asking Him to help each of you face conflict with an open mind and heart, always seeking an outcome that is best for everyone involved.

SESSION THREE: STAND DOWN

The Point: I don't have to get my way to solve a conflict.

The Passage: Genesis 13:1-18

The Setting: The time in Egypt had been profitable to Abram. His nephew, Lot, had remained with him but between Abram and Lot, there was not enough land for all their livestock. This led to quarrels among the herdsmen. Abram gave Lot his choice of land. Lot chose the land to the east—the land that looked better—and Abram occupied the land of Canaan. The land Lot chose eventually returned to Abram and his descendants.

Icebreaker: As a kid, what made you call "Mine!" most often?

Optional activity: Lead your group through a problem-solving scenario by offering them a bag of candy. Choose a bag that has individually-wrapped pieces of candy (chocolates will work as well) and that contains more pieces than the number of people in the group. Direct group members to divide all the candy among themselves and see how they solve the problem of not being able to divide things evenly. When finished, use the following questions to unpack the experience:

- How much pressure do you typically feel to do things "fairly"?

- How does our culture teach us to respond when our desires come in conflict with fairness?

- How does God's Word teach us to respond?

Video Summary: Ron opens his video message by introducing the focal passage of Scripture for this session—Genesis 13:1-18. He talks a little about Lot and Abram and the division of land between them and how things could have gotten uncomfortable if Abram had not acted out of his faith and the wisdom given him by God. Lot chose the better land and received instant reward but ultimately found himself in trouble. Abram extended grace and God blessed him for that in the end.

WATCH THE DVD SEGMENT FOR SESSION 3, THEN USE THE FOLLOWING QUESTIONS TO TRANSITION INTO THE STUDY.

- Ron challenges us to think: perhaps Lot reasoned that he deserved the best land because Abram was the one who had received God's anointing. But what if Abram had decided that because of that very anointing he was the one who deserved the best land and acted on that? How do you think things might have turned out differently?

- Abram and Lot were very different people. Abram followed God and did things God's way. Lot followed his own way and lived for himself. Do you have trouble following the grace Abram extended to Lot? Explain.

WHAT DOES THE BIBLE SAY?

ASK FOR A VOLUNTEER TO READ ALOUD GENESIS 13:1-18.
Response: What's your initial reaction to these verses?

- What questions do you have about Abram's actions toward Lot?

- What new application do you hope to get from this passage?

TURN THE GROUP'S ATTENTION TO GENESIS 13:1-7.
QUESTION 1: When has a time of worship changed your perspective or course of action?

This is an application question that requires group members to recall a worship experience that brought about a change in their behavior. This question provides a great opportunity for group members to share stories of worship experiences that made a significant impact in their lives. Make time for those stories if they come.

Optional follow-up: How do you worship in personal devotional time?

MOVE TO GENESIS 13:8-13.

QUESTION 2: What keeps us from approaching conflict the way Abram did?

This self-revelation question is designed to give group members an opportunity to examine the things that may be keeping them from facing conflict situations in a healthy way. As individuals share their own roadblocks, encourage the rest of the group to listen and consider whether those things might be present in their own lives as well.

> *Optional follow-up:* What are the consequences of *not* approaching conflict as Abram did?

QUESTION 3: How could your willingness to take the short end of the stick impact your relationships?

This question challenges group members to examine what good could come from being willing to step back and consider when it's best to let the battle go.

> *Optional activity:* Direct group members to the activity labeled "The Circumstance; My Choice." Ask for at least one volunteer to respond to each of the three questions.

CONTINUE WITH GENESIS 13:14-18.

QUESTION 4: What choices to stand down have you made that had unexpected results?

This application question may result in another opportunity for group members to share their stories.

> *Optional follow-up:* Are you currently involved in any situations that would benefit from a choice to stand down? Explain.

Note: The following question does not appear in the group member book. Use it in your group discussion as time allows.

QUESTION 5: What do you feel like you give up if you give in?

This question gives group members an opportunity to acknowledge the things that make them resistant to compromise in a conflict situation as well as honestly look at what is most important.

LIVE IT OUT

Conflict happens. Guide group members to consider a plan for handling conflict in a way that honors God.

- **Focus on the end result.** Evaluate what really matters in the long run and work toward it.

- **Humble yourself.** Listen to the other person and speak with humility.

- **Heal a relationship.** Seek out someone who's been a casualty of a conflict with you and reconcile with that person.

Challenge: Remind group members that there are battles to fight and battles to let go of. Encourage them to always approach conflict situations with the end in mind—from a position of what matters most in the end — and to be willing to work toward making that happen. Suggest that members journal about any conflicts that arise during the week when they realize the best solution is for them to stand down.

Pray: Ask for prayer requests and ask group members to pray for the different requests as intercessors. As the leader, close the prayer time by asking the Lord to help each of you consider "not only his own interests, but also the interests of others" (Phil. 2:4).

The Point: Never compromise when the issue is a matter of biblical right and wrong.

The Passage: Galatians 2:1-14

The Setting: In response to opposition from some of the people in the Galatian churches, Paul defended his ministry to the Gentiles. He explained that even the leaders in Jerusalem affirmed his ministry to the Gentiles and the truth that the gospel is for all people, free from any Jewish rules or rituals. This was an uncompromising truth that led Paul to confront Peter when Peter's hypocritical actions made a distinction between Jews and Gentiles.

Icebreaker: When have you drawn a line in the sand?

> ***Optional follow-up:*** How do you typically react when others draw a line in the sand and ask you not to cross?

> ***Optional activity:*** Add a visual layer to the icebreaker experience by playing one or more clips from movies or TV shows where characters take a strong stand.

Video Summary: This week Ron begins by pointing out that we pick up in the passage 14 years after Paul's conversion. Paul and Barnabas were called by God to reach the Gentiles in Antioch. At this time there were great things happening among the Christians in Antioch. But these new Christians in Antioch caused some concerned for the believers in Jerusalem. Fifteen years earlier, Jerusalem was where all the excitement was taking place, but things were different now. Antioch was the cutting edge of what God was doing in the world.

WATCH THE DVD SEGMENT FOR SESSION 4, THEN USE THE FOLLOWING QUESTIONS TO TRANSITION INTO THE STUDY.

- Ron talks about how changes made in churches today by younger generations can sometimes be unsettling to older generations. How do we determine the difference between things that are truth—therefore worth taking a stand on—and those which are merely issues of preference?

WHAT DOES THE BIBLE SAY?

ASK FOR A VOLUNTEER TO READ ALOUD GALATIANS 2:1-14.
Response: What's your initial reaction to these verses?

- What questions do you have about these verses?

- What new application do you hope to get from this passage about how to resist pressure and base your actions on the Truth?

TURN THE GROUP'S ATTENTION TO GALATIANS 2:1-5.
QUESTION 1: How would you describe the freedom we have in Christ?

> ***Optional follow-up:*** What ideas or images come to mind when you hear the word *freedom*?

MOVE TO GALATIANS 2:6-10.
QUESTION 2: Why was it significant that these men gave Paul their support and approval?

By looking at Paul's experience, this application question will help group members examine how important it is to have support and approval from other believers when they are trying to stand strong for what they believe. As the leader, encourage them to also consider their role and responsibility in supporting others in similar situations.

> ***Optional follow-up using Acts 9:1-6:*** Paul persecuted the church before becoming a servant of Jesus, and yet he was welcomed years later by church leaders. How can we as a group (and as a church) welcome and support those who are new to the faith?

CONTINUE WITH GALATIANS 2:11-14.

QUESTION 3: How do you know whether you're standing your ground on biblical principles or personal preferences?

This question is designed to get group members to closely examine the filters they use to make decisions about how they will handle conflict situations.

> ***Optional follow-up:*** How can we support each other as a group when these questions come up?

QUESTION 4: What role does love play in how you stand your ground?

This question helps group members shift from a more personal focus to look at how standing their ground can and will affect others and why that is important.

Optional activity: Direct participants to the activity titled "The Conflict of Compromise." Ask for volunteers to share their response to one of the three options.

Note: The following question does not appear in the group member book. Use it in your group discussion as time allows.

QUESTION 5: Have you ever found yourself in a conflict situation that led you to question something that had previously been a "non-negotiable" for you? Explain.

This question will give group members an opportunity to share stories as well as examine situations that have the potential to push them in a direction of compromise they might regret later. You may hear answers like protection of an important relationship, concern over what someone else thinks, desire to make a good impression, etc.

LIVE IT OUT

Lead group members to consider these three actions when conflict becomes a matter of biblical right and wrong.

- **Draw the line in the sand.** Determine what is non-negotiable and make sure it is consistent with biblical teaching.
- **Practice what you preach.** If you're asking someone to live according to a biblical principle, be certain they can see it in your life.
- **Call others to stand with you.** Mentor and disciple someone else in embracing biblical teaching.

Challenge: Last week you discussed times when it makes more sense to stand down during a conflict, but this week you've discussed conflict situations that involve non-negotiables—matters of biblical right and wrong. Encourage group members to spend some time this week asking the Lord to show them the things in their lives that have the potential to tempt them to compromise what they have previously considered uncompromisable.

Pray: Ask for prayer requests and ask group members to pray for the different requests as intercessors. As the leader, close the prayer time by asking the Lord to help each of you stay strong in conflict when it comes down to a matter that requires you to stand up for what is right and true. Ask Him to also help you recognize opportunities and be willing to step up to support others when they are called to take a stand.

The Point: Step in to keep a bad situation from getting worse.

The Passage: 1 Samuel 24:14-17,23-28,32-35

The Setting: While David was in the wilderness, he sought support from Nabal, for whom David's men had provided protection. When Nabal refused, David became very angry and set out for revenge. Nabal's wife Abigail intervened with both wisdom and diplomacy, keeping the conflict from becoming disastrous.

Icebreaker: How do you respond when you hear, "It's none of your business"?

> *Optional follow-up:* When do you typically hear those words?

> *Optional follow-up:* What emotions do you experience when you hear those words?

Video Summary: This week Ron talks about David's grief over the death of Samuel. Samuel was David's spiritual father, and David felt great loss. Nabal, who David sought out for support for his men, was a wealthy man who had plenty to share, but his success led to selfishness rather than generosity. David's reaction to Nabal was likely influenced by the loss he had experienced. He was very angry with Nabal's refusal to provide the support he asked for, but the Lord sent a peacemaker in Abigail. She was willing to take a risk, step in, and do the right thing.

WATCH THE DVD SEGMENT FOR SESSION 5, THEN USE THE FOLLOWING QUESTIONS TO TRANSITION INTO THE STUDY.

- How do you think selfishness contributes to conflict?

- Ron also talked about how important peacemakers—like Abigail—can be in conflict situations. In what ways can we be peacemakers?

WHAT DOES THE BIBLE SAY?

ASK FOR A VOLUNTEER TO READ ALOUD 1 SAMUEL 25:14-17,23-28,32-35.
Response: What's your initial reaction to these verses?

- What questions do you have about these verses?

- What new application do you hope to get from this passage?

TURN THE GROUP'S ATTENTION TO 1 SAMUEL 25:14-17.
QUESTION 1: What's the difference between tattling and giving someone information to keep a bad situation from becoming worse?

> *Optional follow-up:* What's your impression of the servant's actions and decisions in this story?

MOVE TO 1 SAMUEL 25:23-28.
QUESTION 2: What prevents us from stopping a "train wreck" in someone's life?

> *Optional follow-up:* When have you confronted someone in order to prevent a train wreck?

QUESTION 3: What does Abigail's story teach us about how to step in?

This question allows group members to use Abigail's example to help define what stepping in appropriately looks like, why they would step in, when to step in, and how best to handle stepping in.

> ***Optional activity:*** Direct participants to the activity labeled "Step In … Or Step Away." Ask for several volunteers to share their responses.

CONTINUE WITH 1 SAMUEL 25:32-35.

QUESTION 4: What does it take to step in and get involved?

As group members consider this question, encourage them to think of a situation from their own lives where they stepped in or wished they had stepped in. This question will give them an opportunity to examine what kind of commitment is involved in stepping in as well as the potential risks that could be involved.

> ***Optional follow-up:*** When have you wished someone would step in and get involved in a dilemma you were facing?

Note: The following question does not appear in the group member book. Use it in your group discussion as time allows.

QUESTION 5: When did someone step in and get involved when you were headed toward a bad decision? How did you respond?

This application question is designed to help group members use their own personal experiences to identify how important it is to have others in our lives who are willing to step in and say the hard things when we need to hear them. Encourage group members to consider their responsibility to do the same for others as well.

LIVE IT OUT

Lead group members to consider these three actions when deciding whether or not to step in.

- **Give permission.** Give someone permission to step in if you are about to make a bad decision.

- **Seek advice.** If you're not sure if you should step into someone else's problem, ask the advice of someone you trust.

- **Intervene diplomatically.** Say what needs to be said with humility and respect.

Challenge: Encourage group members to have some deeper conversations about this subject this week with their closest family and friends. Ask, "Have you ever felt like I was making a bad decision and wanted to step in?" And, "What would you want me to do if I felt like you were making a bad decision? How would you like me to approach that conversation?"

Pray: Ask for prayer requests and ask group members to pray for the different requests as intercessors. As the leader, close the prayer time by asking the Lord to guide each of you and help you know when you need to step in and be honest with someone who is heading in a bad direction. Also ask Him to help you be open to others who feel the need to step into your lives in the same way.

The Point: God is at work even in the midst of conflict.

The Passage: Genesis 37:5-8, 26-28; 50:15-21

The Setting: Favoritism, hatred, and envy defined the family of Jacob. The older sons of Jacob hated Joseph so much that they wanted to kill him. They chose instead to profit from their hatred, and they sold Joseph. From the brothers' perspective, it seemed they were done with their brother. But years later, they found themselves standing before Joseph as he served as the second-in-command in Egypt. Joseph forgave his brothers because he saw that God was at work through all that transpired.

Icebreaker: When have you seen the silver lining in a difficult situation?

> *Optional follow-up:* What attitudes or obstacles prevent us from seeing silver linings when available?

> *Optional activity:* Add another layer to the icebreaker experience by turning out the lights and encouraging participants to discuss the above questions in darkness. Ask the following unpacking questions when those discussions have ended:

> - What is it about darkness that makes us uncomfortable or afraid?
> - What emotions do you experience when you can't see what's going on in the world around you?
> - What emotions do you experience when you don't understand what God is doing in your life?

Video Summary: In this week's video, Ron shares the story of Ronald Cotton who was mistakenly identified by Jennifer Thompson as the man who raped her. He was sentenced to prison but later found innocent and released. Cotton forgave Thompson. In our Scripture passage for today, we see that just as Cotton was able to forgive Thompson, Joseph forgave his brothers for all they had done to him. In both situations there was a choice—they could forgive or seek revenge.

WATCH THE DVD SEGMENT FOR SESSION 6, THEN USE THE FOLLOWING QUESTIONS TO TRANSITION INTO THE STUDY.

- How can Joseph's story bring restoration to your life?
- Ron also talks about how uncovering the pain of conflict—acknowledging our feelings of guilt and pain and choosing to forgive—can lead to real healing in our lives. In what ways have you known this to be true in your life?

WHAT DOES THE BIBLE SAY?

ASK FOR A VOLUNTEER TO READ ALOUD GENESIS 37:5-8,26-28; 50:15-21.

Response: What's your initial reaction to these verses?

- What questions do you have about understanding God's plan in the midst of your conflict?
- What new application do you hope to get from this passage?

TURN THE GROUP'S ATTENTION TO GENESIS 37:5-8.

QUESTION 1: When have you seen behaviors like this fuel the fire of conflict?

This question is designed to give group members an opportunity to use the story of Joseph and his family to share their own stories of conflict. You may hear stories of family conflict, other relationships, work situations, etc. Help members identify specific behaviors in their own stories that might have encouraged conflict.

> *Optional follow-up:* What kinds of behaviors quench the fires of conflict?

MOVE TO GENESIS 37:26-28.
QUESTION 2: How has a conflict shaped your life?

This question provides group members with another chance to share their stories. Allow them to share both positive and negative experiences but challenge them to identify at least one way God was at work in the midst of their conflict.

> *Optional follow-up:* What emotions do you feel when you think about the conflicts you've experienced?

CONTINUE WITH GENESIS 50:15-21.
QUESTION 3: What will help you extend forgiveness when you're wronged?

> *Optional activity:* Direct group members to "The Big Picture" activity. Ask for volunteers to share responses or give members a few moments to write their answers in their books.

QUESTION 4: How can we encourage each other when we struggle to see evidence that God is at work in difficult situations?

This application question will help group members look beyond themselves to see how they can help others see the positive in the midst of a situation that looks painfully negative.

> **Note**: The following question does not appear in the group member book. Use it in your group discussion as time allows.

QUESTION 5: What are some examples of ways God chooses to work in difficult situations?

LIVE IT OUT
Conflict can be draining, but God can use whatever conflict we are facing to bring meaningful results in our lives. Lead group members to consider these three actions that can lead to stronger relationships.

- **Trust.** Even if you can't see God's hand yet, trust that He is at work.
- **Forgive.** Regardless of who's at fault in the conflict, forgive the other person.
- **Call.** Contact someone and let him or her know how God changed you because of your experience with the conflict.

Challenge: Encourage group members to spend some time thinking back on conflict situations when they were unable to recognize God working in the midst of the struggle but can now see He was there. Suggest that they record these experiences in a journal so they can look back at it the next time they find themselves unable to trace God's hand.

Pray: As the leader, close this final session of *When Relationships Collide* in prayer. Ask the Lord to help each of you as you move forward to use the principles you have learned in this study to deal with conflict in a way that is healthy and God-honoring.

WHERE THE BIBLE MEETS LIFE

Bible Studies for Life™ will help you know Christ, live in community, and impact the world around you. If you enjoyed this study, be sure and check out these forthcoming releases.* Six sessions each.

TITLE	RELEASE DATE
Pressure Points *by Chip Henderson*	June 2013
When Relationships Collide *by Ron Edmondson*	June 2013
Do Over: Experience New Life in Christ *by Ben Mandrell*	September 2013
Honest to God: Real Questions Christians Ask *by Robert Jeffress*	September 2013
Let Hope In *by Pete Wilson*	December 2013
Productive: Finding Joy in Work *by Ronnie and Nick Floyd*	December 2013
Resilient Faith: Staying Faithful in the Midst of Suffering *by Mary Jo Sharp*	March 2014
What Is God Like? *by Freddy Cardoza*	March 2014

If your group meets regularly, you might consider Bible Studies for Life as an ongoing series. Available for your entire church—kids, students, and adults—it's a format that will be a more affordable option over time. And you can jump in anytime. For more information, visit **biblestudiesforlife.com**.

biblestudiesforlife.com/smallgroups
800.458.2772